WEBSITE: _____

USERNAME: _____

PASSWORD: _____

NOTES: _____

_____

WEBSITE: _____

USERNAME: _____

PASSWORD: _____

NOTES: _____

_____

WEBSITE: _____

USERNAME: _____

PASSWORD: _____

NOTES _____

A

WEBSITE:

USERNAME:

PASSWORD:

NOTES:

WEBSITE:

USERNAME:

PASSWORD:

NOTES:

WEBSITE:

USERNAME:

PASSWORD:

NOTES

A

WEBSITE:

USERNAME:

PASSWORD:

NOTES:

WEBSITE:

USERNAME:

PASSWORD:

NOTES:

WEBSITE:

USERNAME:

PASSWORD:

NOTES

A

WEBSITE:

USERNAME:

PASSWORD:

NOTES:

WEBSITE:

USERNAME:

PASSWORD:

NOTES:

WEBSITE:

USERNAME:

PASSWORD:

NOTES

B

WEBSITE:

USERNAME:

PASSWORD:

NOTES:

WEBSITE:

USERNAME:

PASSWORD:

NOTES:

WEBSITE:

USERNAME:

PASSWORD:

NOTES

B

WEBSITE:

USERNAME:

PASSWORD:

NOTES:

WEBSITE:

USERNAME:

PASSWORD:

NOTES:

WEBSITE:

USERNAME:

PASSWORD:

NOTES

B

WEBSITE:

USERNAME:

PASSWORD:

NOTES:

WEBSITE:

USERNAME:

PASSWORD:

NOTES:

WEBSITE:

USERNAME:

PASSWORD:

NOTES

B

WEBSITE:

USERNAME:

PASSWORD:

NOTES:

WEBSITE:

USERNAME:

PASSWORD:

NOTES:

WEBSITE:

USERNAME:

PASSWORD:

NOTES

C

WEBSITE:

USERNAME:

PASSWORD:

NOTES:

WEBSITE:

USERNAME:

PASSWORD:

NOTES:

WEBSITE:

USERNAME:

PASSWORD:

NOTES

C

WEBSITE:

USERNAME:

PASSWORD:

NOTES:

WEBSITE:

USERNAME:

PASSWORD:

NOTES:

WEBSITE:

USERNAME:

PASSWORD:

NOTES

C

WEBSITE: _____

USERNAME: _____

PASSWORD: _____

NOTES: _____

_____

WEBSITE: _____

USERNAME: _____

PASSWORD: _____

NOTES: _____

_____

WEBSITE: _____

USERNAME: _____

PASSWORD: _____

NOTES _____

C

WEBSITE: _____

USERNAME: _____

PASSWORD: _____

NOTES: _____

_____

WEBSITE: _____

USERNAME: _____

PASSWORD: _____

NOTES: _____

_____

WEBSITE: _____

USERNAME: _____

PASSWORD: _____

NOTES _____

D

WEBSITE:

USERNAME:

PASSWORD:

NOTES:

WEBSITE:

USERNAME:

PASSWORD:

NOTES:

WEBSITE:

USERNAME:

PASSWORD:

NOTES

D

WEBSITE:

USERNAME:

PASSWORD:

NOTES:

WEBSITE:

USERNAME:

PASSWORD:

NOTES:

WEBSITE:

USERNAME:

PASSWORD:

NOTES

D

WEBSITE:

USERNAME:

PASSWORD:

NOTES:

WEBSITE:

USERNAME:

PASSWORD:

NOTES:

WEBSITE:

USERNAME:

PASSWORD:

NOTES

D

WEBSITE:

USERNAME:

PASSWORD:

NOTES:

WEBSITE:

USERNAME:

PASSWORD:

NOTES:

WEBSITE:

USERNAME:

PASSWORD:

NOTES

E

WEBSITE:

USERNAME:

PASSWORD:

NOTES:

WEBSITE:

USERNAME:

PASSWORD:

NOTES:

WEBSITE:

USERNAME:

PASSWORD:

NOTES

E

WEBSITE:

USERNAME:

PASSWORD:

NOTES:

WEBSITE:

USERNAME:

PASSWORD:

NOTES:

WEBSITE:

USERNAME:

PASSWORD:

NOTES

E

WEBSITE: _____

USERNAME: _____

PASSWORD: _____

NOTES: _____

_____

WEBSITE: _____

USERNAME: _____

PASSWORD: _____

NOTES: _____

_____

WEBSITE: _____

USERNAME: _____

PASSWORD: _____

NOTES _____

E

WEBSITE:

USERNAME:

PASSWORD:

NOTES:

WEBSITE:

USERNAME:

PASSWORD:

NOTES:

WEBSITE:

USERNAME:

PASSWORD:

NOTES

F

WEBSITE:

USERNAME:

PASSWORD:

NOTES:

WEBSITE:

USERNAME:

PASSWORD:

NOTES:

WEBSITE:

USERNAME:

PASSWORD:

NOTES

F

WEBSITE:

USERNAME:

PASSWORD:

NOTES:

WEBSITE:

USERNAME:

PASSWORD:

NOTES:

WEBSITE:

USERNAME:

PASSWORD:

NOTES

F

WEBSITE: _____

USERNAME: _____

PASSWORD: _____

NOTES: _____

_____

WEBSITE: _____

USERNAME: _____

PASSWORD: _____

NOTES: _____

_____

WEBSITE: _____

USERNAME: _____

PASSWORD: _____

NOTES _____

F

WEBSITE: _____

USERNAME: _____

PASSWORD: _____

NOTES: _____

_____

WEBSITE: _____

USERNAME: _____

PASSWORD: _____

NOTES: _____

_____

WEBSITE: _____

USERNAME: _____

PASSWORD: _____

NOTES _____

G

WEBSITE:

USERNAME:

PASSWORD:

NOTES:

WEBSITE:

USERNAME:

PASSWORD:

NOTES:

WEBSITE:

USERNAME:

PASSWORD:

NOTES

G

WEBSITE:

USERNAME:

PASSWORD:

NOTES:

WEBSITE:

USERNAME:

PASSWORD:

NOTES:

WEBSITE:

USERNAME:

PASSWORD:

NOTES

G

WEBSITE:

USERNAME:

PASSWORD:

NOTES:

WEBSITE:

USERNAME:

PASSWORD:

NOTES:

WEBSITE:

USERNAME:

PASSWORD:

NOTES

G

WEBSITE:

USERNAME:

PASSWORD:

NOTES:

WEBSITE:

USERNAME:

PASSWORD:

NOTES:

WEBSITE:

USERNAME:

PASSWORD:

NOTES

H

WEBSITE:

USERNAME:

PASSWORD:

NOTES:

WEBSITE:

USERNAME:

PASSWORD:

NOTES:

WEBSITE:

USERNAME:

PASSWORD:

NOTES

H

WEBSITE:

USERNAME:

PASSWORD:

NOTES:

WEBSITE:

USERNAME:

PASSWORD:

NOTES:

WEBSITE:

USERNAME:

PASSWORD:

NOTES

H

WEBSITE:

USERNAME:

PASSWORD:

NOTES:

WEBSITE:

USERNAME:

PASSWORD:

NOTES:

WEBSITE:

USERNAME:

PASSWORD:

NOTES

H

WEBSITE:

USERNAME:

PASSWORD:

NOTES:

WEBSITE:

USERNAME:

PASSWORD:

NOTES:

WEBSITE:

USERNAME:

PASSWORD:

NOTES

I

WEBSITE:

USERNAME:

PASSWORD:

NOTES:

WEBSITE:

USERNAME:

PASSWORD:

NOTES:

WEBSITE:

USERNAME:

PASSWORD:

NOTES

I

WEBSITE:

USERNAME:

PASSWORD:

NOTES:

WEBSITE:

USERNAME:

PASSWORD:

NOTES:

WEBSITE:

USERNAME:

PASSWORD:

NOTES

I

WEBSITE:

USERNAME:

PASSWORD:

NOTES:

WEBSITE:

USERNAME:

PASSWORD:

NOTES:

WEBSITE:

USERNAME:

PASSWORD:

NOTES

I

WEBSITE:

USERNAME:

PASSWORD:

NOTES:

WEBSITE:

USERNAME:

PASSWORD:

NOTES:

WEBSITE:

USERNAME:

PASSWORD:

NOTES

J

WEBSITE:

USERNAME:

PASSWORD:

NOTES:

WEBSITE:

USERNAME:

PASSWORD:

NOTES:

WEBSITE:

USERNAME:

PASSWORD:

NOTES

J

WEBSITE:

USERNAME:

PASSWORD:

NOTES:

WEBSITE:

USERNAME:

PASSWORD:

NOTES:

WEBSITE:

USERNAME:

PASSWORD:

NOTES

J

WEBSITE:

USERNAME:

PASSWORD:

NOTES:

WEBSITE:

USERNAME:

PASSWORD:

NOTES:

WEBSITE:

USERNAME:

PASSWORD:

NOTES

J

WEBSITE:

USERNAME:

PASSWORD:

NOTES:

WEBSITE:

USERNAME:

PASSWORD:

NOTES:

WEBSITE:

USERNAME:

PASSWORD:

NOTES

K

WEBSITE:

USERNAME:

PASSWORD:

NOTES:

WEBSITE:

USERNAME:

PASSWORD:

NOTES:

WEBSITE:

USERNAME:

PASSWORD:

NOTES

K

WEBSITE:

USERNAME:

PASSWORD:

NOTES:

WEBSITE:

USERNAME:

PASSWORD:

NOTES:

WEBSITE:

USERNAME:

PASSWORD:

NOTES

K

WEBSITE: _____

USERNAME: _____

PASSWORD: _____

NOTES: _____

_____

WEBSITE: _____

USERNAME: _____

PASSWORD: _____

NOTES: _____

_____

WEBSITE: _____

USERNAME: _____

PASSWORD: _____

NOTES _____

K

WEBSITE:

USERNAME:

PASSWORD:

NOTES:

WEBSITE:

USERNAME:

PASSWORD:

NOTES:

WEBSITE:

USERNAME:

PASSWORD:

NOTES

L

WEBSITE:

USERNAME:

PASSWORD:

NOTES:

WEBSITE:

USERNAME:

PASSWORD:

NOTES:

WEBSITE:

USERNAME:

PASSWORD:

NOTES

L

WEBSITE: _____

USERNAME: _____

PASSWORD: _____

NOTES: _____

_____

WEBSITE: _____

USERNAME: _____

PASSWORD: _____

NOTES: _____

_____

WEBSITE: _____

USERNAME: _____

PASSWORD: _____

NOTES _____

L

WEBSITE:

USERNAME:

PASSWORD:

NOTES:

WEBSITE:

USERNAME:

PASSWORD:

NOTES:

WEBSITE:

USERNAME:

PASSWORD:

NOTES

L

WEBSITE:

USERNAME:

PASSWORD:

NOTES:

WEBSITE:

USERNAME:

PASSWORD:

NOTES:

WEBSITE:

USERNAME:

PASSWORD:

NOTES

M

WEBSITE:

USERNAME:

PASSWORD:

NOTES:

WEBSITE:

USERNAME:

PASSWORD:

NOTES:

WEBSITE:

USERNAME:

PASSWORD:

NOTES

M

WEBSITE:

USERNAME:

PASSWORD:

NOTES:

WEBSITE:

USERNAME:

PASSWORD:

NOTES:

WEBSITE:

USERNAME:

PASSWORD:

NOTES

M

WEBSITE:

USERNAME:

PASSWORD:

NOTES:

WEBSITE:

USERNAME:

PASSWORD:

NOTES:

WEBSITE:

USERNAME:

PASSWORD:

NOTES

M

WEBSITE:

USERNAME:

PASSWORD:

NOTES:

WEBSITE:

USERNAME:

PASSWORD:

NOTES:

WEBSITE:

USERNAME:

PASSWORD:

NOTES

N

WEBSITE: _____

USERNAME: _____

PASSWORD: _____

NOTES: _____

_____

WEBSITE: _____

USERNAME: _____

PASSWORD: _____

NOTES: _____

_____

WEBSITE: _____

USERNAME: _____

PASSWORD: _____

NOTES _____

N

WEBSITE:

USERNAME:

PASSWORD:

NOTES:

WEBSITE:

USERNAME:

PASSWORD:

NOTES:

WEBSITE:

USERNAME:

PASSWORD:

NOTES

N

WEBSITE:

USERNAME:

PASSWORD:

NOTES:

WEBSITE:

USERNAME:

PASSWORD:

NOTES:

WEBSITE:

USERNAME:

PASSWORD:

NOTES

N

WEBSITE:

USERNAME:

PASSWORD:

NOTES:

WEBSITE:

USERNAME:

PASSWORD:

NOTES:

WEBSITE:

USERNAME:

PASSWORD:

NOTES

O

WEBSITE:

USERNAME:

PASSWORD:

NOTES:

WEBSITE:

USERNAME:

PASSWORD:

NOTES:

WEBSITE:

USERNAME:

PASSWORD:

NOTES

O

WEBSITE:

USERNAME:

PASSWORD:

NOTES:

WEBSITE:

USERNAME:

PASSWORD:

NOTES:

WEBSITE:

USERNAME:

PASSWORD:

NOTES

O

WEBSITE:

USERNAME:

PASSWORD:

NOTES:

WEBSITE:

USERNAME:

PASSWORD:

NOTES:

WEBSITE:

USERNAME:

PASSWORD:

NOTES

O

WEBSITE: _____

USERNAME: _____

PASSWORD: _____

NOTES: _____

_____

WEBSITE: _____

USERNAME: _____

PASSWORD: _____

NOTES: _____

_____

WEBSITE: _____

USERNAME: _____

PASSWORD: _____

NOTES _____

P

WEBSITE:

USERNAME:

PASSWORD:

NOTES:

WEBSITE:

USERNAME:

PASSWORD:

NOTES:

WEBSITE:

USERNAME:

PASSWORD:

NOTES

P

WEBSITE:

USERNAME:

PASSWORD:

NOTES:

WEBSITE:

USERNAME:

PASSWORD:

NOTES:

WEBSITE:

USERNAME:

PASSWORD:

NOTES

P

WEBSITE: _____

USERNAME: _____

PASSWORD: _____

NOTES: _____

_____

WEBSITE: _____

USERNAME: _____

PASSWORD: _____

NOTES: _____

_____

WEBSITE: _____

USERNAME: _____

PASSWORD: _____

NOTES _____

P

WEBSITE: _____

USERNAME: _____

PASSWORD: _____

NOTES: _____

_____

WEBSITE: _____

USERNAME: _____

PASSWORD: _____

NOTES: _____

_____

WEBSITE: _____

USERNAME: _____

PASSWORD: _____

NOTES _____

Q

WEBSITE:

USERNAME:

PASSWORD:

NOTES:

WEBSITE:

USERNAME:

PASSWORD:

NOTES:

WEBSITE:

USERNAME:

PASSWORD:

NOTES

Q

WEBSITE: _____

USERNAME: _____

PASSWORD: _____

NOTES: _____

_____

WEBSITE: _____

USERNAME: _____

PASSWORD: _____

NOTES: _____

_____

WEBSITE: _____

USERNAME: _____

PASSWORD: _____

NOTES _____

Q

WEBSITE: _____

USERNAME: _____

PASSWORD: _____

NOTES: _____

_____

WEBSITE: _____

USERNAME: _____

PASSWORD: _____

NOTES: _____

_____

WEBSITE: _____

USERNAME: _____

PASSWORD: _____

NOTES _____

Q

WEBSITE:

USERNAME:

PASSWORD:

NOTES:

WEBSITE:

USERNAME:

PASSWORD:

NOTES:

WEBSITE:

USERNAME:

PASSWORD:

NOTES

R

WEBSITE:

USERNAME:

PASSWORD:

NOTES:

WEBSITE:

USERNAME:

PASSWORD:

NOTES:

WEBSITE:

USERNAME:

PASSWORD:

NOTES

R

WEBSITE:

USERNAME:

PASSWORD:

NOTES:

WEBSITE:

USERNAME:

PASSWORD:

NOTES:

WEBSITE:

USERNAME:

PASSWORD:

NOTES

R

WEBSITE:

USERNAME:

PASSWORD:

NOTES:

WEBSITE:

USERNAME:

PASSWORD:

NOTES:

WEBSITE:

USERNAME:

PASSWORD:

NOTES

R

WEBSITE: _____

USERNAME: _____

PASSWORD: _____

NOTES: _____

_____

WEBSITE: _____

USERNAME: _____

PASSWORD: _____

NOTES: _____

_____

WEBSITE: _____

USERNAME: _____

PASSWORD: _____

NOTES _____

S

WEBSITE:

USERNAME:

PASSWORD:

NOTES:

WEBSITE:

USERNAME:

PASSWORD:

NOTES:

WEBSITE:

USERNAME:

PASSWORD:

NOTES

S

WEBSITE:

USERNAME:

PASSWORD:

NOTES:

WEBSITE:

USERNAME:

PASSWORD:

NOTES:

WEBSITE:

USERNAME:

PASSWORD:

NOTES

S

WEBSITE:

USERNAME:

PASSWORD:

NOTES:

WEBSITE:

USERNAME:

PASSWORD:

NOTES:

WEBSITE:

USERNAME:

PASSWORD:

NOTES

S

WEBSITE:

USERNAME:

PASSWORD:

NOTES:

WEBSITE:

USERNAME:

PASSWORD:

NOTES:

WEBSITE:

USERNAME:

PASSWORD:

NOTES

T

WEBSITE:

USERNAME:

PASSWORD:

NOTES:

WEBSITE:

USERNAME:

PASSWORD:

NOTES:

WEBSITE:

USERNAME:

PASSWORD:

NOTES

T

WEBSITE: _____

USERNAME: _____

PASSWORD: _____

NOTES: _____

_____

WEBSITE: _____

USERNAME: _____

PASSWORD: _____

NOTES: _____

_____

WEBSITE: _____

USERNAME: _____

PASSWORD: _____

NOTES _____

T

WEBSITE:

USERNAME:

PASSWORD:

NOTES:

WEBSITE:

USERNAME:

PASSWORD:

NOTES:

WEBSITE:

USERNAME:

PASSWORD:

NOTES

T

WEBSITE:

USERNAME:

PASSWORD:

NOTES:

WEBSITE:

USERNAME:

PASSWORD:

NOTES:

WEBSITE:

USERNAME:

PASSWORD:

NOTES

U

WEBSITE:

USERNAME:

PASSWORD:

NOTES:

WEBSITE:

USERNAME:

PASSWORD:

NOTES:

WEBSITE:

USERNAME:

PASSWORD:

NOTES

U

WEBSITE:

USERNAME:

PASSWORD:

NOTES:

WEBSITE:

USERNAME:

PASSWORD:

NOTES:

WEBSITE:

USERNAME:

PASSWORD:

NOTES

U

WEBSITE:

USERNAME:

PASSWORD:

NOTES:

WEBSITE:

USERNAME:

PASSWORD:

NOTES:

WEBSITE:

USERNAME:

PASSWORD:

NOTES

U

WEBSITE:

USERNAME:

PASSWORD:

NOTES:

WEBSITE:

USERNAME:

PASSWORD:

NOTES:

WEBSITE:

USERNAME:

PASSWORD:

NOTES

V

WEBSITE:

USERNAME:

PASSWORD:

NOTES:

WEBSITE:

USERNAME:

PASSWORD:

NOTES:

WEBSITE:

USERNAME:

PASSWORD:

NOTES

V

WEBSITE:

USERNAME:

PASSWORD:

NOTES:

WEBSITE:

USERNAME:

PASSWORD:

NOTES:

WEBSITE:

USERNAME:

PASSWORD:

NOTES

V

WEBSITE:

USERNAME:

PASSWORD:

NOTES:

WEBSITE:

USERNAME:

PASSWORD:

NOTES:

WEBSITE:

USERNAME:

PASSWORD:

NOTES

V

WEBSITE:

USERNAME:

PASSWORD:

NOTES:

WEBSITE:

USERNAME:

PASSWORD:

NOTES:

WEBSITE:

USERNAME:

PASSWORD:

NOTES

W

WEBSITE: _____

USERNAME: _____

PASSWORD: _____

NOTES: _____

_____

WEBSITE: _____

USERNAME: _____

PASSWORD: _____

NOTES: _____

_____

WEBSITE: _____

USERNAME: _____

PASSWORD: _____

NOTES _____

W

WEBSITE: _____

USERNAME: _____

PASSWORD: _____

NOTES: _____

_____

WEBSITE: _____

USERNAME: _____

PASSWORD: _____

NOTES: _____

_____

WEBSITE: _____

USERNAME: _____

PASSWORD: _____

NOTES _____

W

WEBSITE:

USERNAME:

PASSWORD:

NOTES:

WEBSITE:

USERNAME:

PASSWORD:

NOTES:

WEBSITE:

USERNAME:

PASSWORD:

NOTES

W

WEBSITE:

USERNAME:

PASSWORD:

NOTES:

WEBSITE:

USERNAME:

PASSWORD:

NOTES:

WEBSITE:

USERNAME:

PASSWORD:

NOTES

X

WEBSITE:

USERNAME:

PASSWORD:

NOTES:

WEBSITE:

USERNAME:

PASSWORD:

NOTES:

WEBSITE:

USERNAME:

PASSWORD:

NOTES

X

WEBSITE:

USERNAME:

PASSWORD:

NOTES:

WEBSITE:

USERNAME:

PASSWORD:

NOTES:

WEBSITE:

USERNAME:

PASSWORD:

NOTES

X

WEBSITE:

USERNAME:

PASSWORD:

NOTES:

WEBSITE:

USERNAME:

PASSWORD:

NOTES:

WEBSITE:

USERNAME:

PASSWORD:

NOTES

X

WEBSITE: _____

USERNAME: _____

PASSWORD: _____

NOTES: _____

_____

WEBSITE: _____

USERNAME: _____

PASSWORD: _____

NOTES: _____

_____

WEBSITE: _____

USERNAME: _____

PASSWORD: _____

NOTES _____

Y

WEBSITE:

USERNAME:

PASSWORD:

NOTES:

WEBSITE:

USERNAME:

PASSWORD:

NOTES:

WEBSITE:

USERNAME:

PASSWORD:

NOTES

Y

WEBSITE:

USERNAME:

PASSWORD:

NOTES:

WEBSITE:

USERNAME:

PASSWORD:

NOTES:

WEBSITE:

USERNAME:

PASSWORD:

NOTES

Y

WEBSITE: _____

USERNAME: _____

PASSWORD: _____

NOTES: _____

_____

WEBSITE: _____

USERNAME: _____

PASSWORD: _____

NOTES: _____

_____

WEBSITE: _____

USERNAME: _____

PASSWORD: _____

NOTES _____

Y

WEBSITE: _____

USERNAME: _____

PASSWORD: _____

NOTES: _____

_____

WEBSITE: _____

USERNAME: _____

PASSWORD: _____

NOTES: _____

_____

WEBSITE: _____

USERNAME: _____

PASSWORD: _____

NOTES _____

Z

WEBSITE:

USERNAME:

PASSWORD:

NOTES:

WEBSITE:

USERNAME:

PASSWORD:

NOTES:

WEBSITE:

USERNAME:

PASSWORD:

NOTES

Z

WEBSITE:

USERNAME:

PASSWORD:

NOTES:

WEBSITE:

USERNAME:

PASSWORD:

NOTES:

WEBSITE:

USERNAME:

PASSWORD:

NOTES

Z

WEBSITE:

USERNAME:

PASSWORD:

NOTES:

WEBSITE:

USERNAME:

PASSWORD:

NOTES:

WEBSITE:

USERNAME:

PASSWORD:

NOTES

Z

WEBSITE:

USERNAME:

PASSWORD:

NOTES:

WEBSITE:

USERNAME:

PASSWORD:

NOTES:

WEBSITE:

USERNAME:

PASSWORD:

NOTES

NOTES

Made in the USA
Monee, IL
15 October 2020

45074505R00066